SPORTSVORSCHRIFT FÜR DAS HEER

THE WEHRMACHT

FITNESS MANUAL

H.Dv. 475

SPORTSVORSCHRIFT FÜR DAS HEER

THE WEHRMACHT

FITNESS MANUAL

Fitness Guidelines for the Army

Translated by Anon

A🦌H

Antelope Hill Publishing

First published in German; October 1, 1938.
Verlag von E.G. Mittler & Sohn / Berlin.

First Published in English, electronically; April 15, 2020.
Printing 2020.
Translated by Anon, as a collaborate effort directed by The Bureau of Memetic Warfare. Printed and distributed with their permission. All rights reserved by them.

Cover art by sswifty.

The publisher can be contacted at
Antelopehillpublishing.com

The role of Antelope Hill in publishing this release is to preserve for the sake of future generation, in physical hardcopy format, this mighty collaborative effort. As such, the greatest of care has been taken to retain the original format of the 1938 Wehrmacht Fitness Manual.

Thank you to the men of The Bureau of Memetic Warfare for granting us the privilege of transitioning this book out of the internet and onto the printed page, ensuring its survival against state and corporate censorship.

Hardcover ISBN-13: 978-1-953730-24-4

Dedication

Every time you accomplish a collaborative goal, you not only hone yourself, you sort out capable men whose competence may lend itself to future and grander accomplishments.

This book is dedicated to what we will build.

⊰ Contents ⊱

Editor's Note

This translation is the result of a truly collaborative effort by young men brought together from far and wide for one purpose: to render into the English language the previously untranslated fitness manual of the Third Reich Wehrmacht. The process was long and the difficulties many: the usual difficulties in translating idiomatic expressions, technical language, niche terms, differences of opinion, waning interest among some early collaborators, and multiple stages of editing, revision, and rewriting; yet we who persevered, as well as our stubbornly determined editors, are satisfied that we have achieved this goal competently. Due to the intended audience of the original text (mostly Wehrmacht officers and drill sergeants, who would then instruct their men in the exercises), the text was rife with technical military terminology, as well as highly specific exercise instructions and terminology, especially in the sections focusing on very technical exercises such as diving and gymnastics. Certain sections also assume a level of pre-existing familiarity with sport and exercise terminology. While we aimed to remain as faithful to the original German as possible, we also wanted the text to be readable and easily understood for the modern English speaker. With this in mind, there are instances where the directness of the translation is sacrificed in order to increase clarity and readability, all while retaining the sense and general meaning of the original text. The end result, we believe, is a readable text in English of great historical interest, an insight into the training and rationale for said training of the soldiers who were widely regarded, even by their enemies, as among the world's best. And even today, with its principles of practical, functional exercise, it lives up to its original purpose as a fitness manual that we believe can be truly useful to any man or group of men dedicated to improving the form and function of their bodies. Now our work as translators is done and yours, as the reader of this manual and practitioner of its principles, can begin.

Authorization

I approve the following fitness guidelines for the army effective as of the 1st October 1938. The inspector of the army school may arrange for non-fundamental corrections.

W. Brauchitsch

⚔ I. Guiding Principals ⚕

Sportive activities raise and preserve the performance of the soldiers body, hardening it like steel - rewarding him with strength, endurance, speed, and agility. Therefore, sport is the foundation of combat training and an indispensable aspect of military service.

.

Sport awakens the offensive spirit, hardens the will, fosters self discipline and thereby supports the education of the soldier into a fighter ready for action.

.

Sport forces discipline and hardens the bond and spirit of the unit. It provides the soldier with relaxation, recreation, and the spark of joy.

⚔ II. Management ⚔

Commander Duties

The company commander is responsible for the sports training of his subordinates. A successful physical education is not possible without good teaching staff; the company commander must therefore take special care that both officers and non-commissioned officers are exemplary in their performance.

The commanders of the regiments, battalions, and divisions monitor the training of the troops by means of inspections, performance tests, and competitions. They make certain that individuals make necessary performance improvements through targeted training and thus that sport is made useful for military purposes. They mandate sports courses for the uniform training of teaching staff. They ensure that the young officers engage in sports themselves.

Sports Officer Duties

The battalion commander is assisted by the sports officer; this officer is to be young and will serve as the head of sports training. His personal performance should be significantly higher than the average performance of the unit - he should have a special disposition for sport, have gained practical experience, and, if possible, participated in a course at an army sports school. He must be able to demonstrate and explain the sporting exercises. His participation in competitions is recommended. His example determines the success of his training.

The sports officer must be trained as an arbitrator and judge proficient in safety regulations and the basic principles of health care. In addition, the sports officer should be familiar with the equipment and space management as well as the facilities of the German Reich Association for Physical Exercise at his location. The officer wears the same uniform as the training unit.

The sports officer's actions are governed by his commander - these include:

- Advising the commander and company commander on organizational and technical questions of training and sports facilities (gymnasium, playing field, swimming pool etc.)

- Provision, maintenance and storage of equipment, installation and maintenance of sports facilities

- Management of training courses for teaching staff

- Organization and execution of sports competitions

- Training management of competition teams

- Management of army sports clubs

- Maintaining contact with the German Reich Association for Physical Exercise and their affiliated associations

- Preparing sports lessons by readying equipment and dividing up the company

- Keeping records of performance tests

- Acting as a referee during competitions

- Accompanying competition teams as captain or quartermaster if no other officer is available

Medical Duties

It is the duty of the military doctor, in close cooperation with the leaders responsible for training in sport, to monitor the troops' state of health, prevent overexertion, and teach the troops about health and hygiene issues.

Training Philosophy

Training shall be based on the existing skills and abilities of the recruits. A simple, informal approach to sporting practice, which avoids any unnecessary drill, awakens spirit and love for sport and encourages training. From the beginning of training, exercises will often take place in squadrons and units in order to stimulate the sports lesson and increase performance.

The demands on the body, corresponding to its state of strength, must be adapted to the preceding performances and balanced with current ability. The training of muscles and internal organs (i.e. cardiovascular system) must go hand in hand.

In order to avoid militarily undesirable one-sidedness, the soldier should demonstrate good average performance in all areas of official sport (to be physically proficient in all areas). In addition, he should be brought to his personal peak performance in one or more areas.

After completion of the recruit training, it is therefore necessary to take a closer look at the abilities of the individual man. Training in top level divisions is often recommended so that soldiers with a good sporting disposition are not hampered in their further training by those with poor performance. Soldiers with particularly good performances, especially non-commissioned officers, can receive further training in voluntary exercises in sports fields that are particularly suited to their inclination and disposition. Soldiers who are preparing for competitions may also receive training opportunities in official sports.

Training Conditions

Physical education lays the foundation for performance and will generally occur via mass instruction through group exercises. Track and field, swimming, boxing, and team games develop the soldier's performance to its utmost.

Sport should be practiced outdoors as much as possible. When the weather is cool, sports training must begin with gymnastics, short runs, or other exercises that warm-up the individual in order to prevent sickness and muscular injuries. The normal outfit is sports pants and footwear. Depending on the weather, sports shirts and protective sports suits (tracksuits) can be added. When practicing intensely, the latter should be discarded even in cold weather. Barefoot training strengthens the feet and is permissible in good weather and in proper ground conditions. During games (handball, etc.) the footwear of the players must be uniform in order to prevent injuries.

Sports training should not be condensed into only one or two days a week, neither should continuous training longer than 1-1.5 hours generally occur. As needed, the doctor can temporarily exempt people in need of care from sport.

Closed rooms must be well ventilated and thoroughly cleaned often. The air must be dust free. It is forbidden to practice sport in occupied stables.

The value of the training hours will increase if enough time is given to rest and clean the body afterwards. After cross-country races this is to be demanded in principle. Short warm showers reduce fatigue and eliminate muscle stiffness.

Regular early morning exercise is only offered where there is otherwise no possibility of regular exercise operations. Its purpose is to stimulate blood flow and revitalize the body in the absence of a full training regimen. A short run and a few minutes of movement exercises are particularly suitable for this purpose. Early morning exercise can never replace sports training aimed at performance.

◄ III. Training Course ►

Sport must be implemented in the training course in a way that supports future training with weapons. The year is split into two training phases:

I. Training Prior to Individual Inspection

II. Training After Individual Inspection

First Year of Service:

I. Phase One

The training areas are "Körperschule" (body school), trail-running (which must take place two times each month with increasing difficulty), and boxing (first training phase, see section IV - E).

Swimming opportunities should be primarily used for the training of regular soldiers and non-swimmers.

II. Phase Two

At the end of April, the trail-running training will finish with standard competitions. The focus of the training should be on boxing, with the intent to ready the participant for free-fighting. (second training phase, see section IV - E).

Körperschule should emphasize jump, throw, and run training. Team sports and swimming may be practiced as fitting.

In the summer months athletics (except trail running), swimming, and team sports are emphasized. Körperschule should be repeated, occasionally emphasizing gymnastics with equipment.

Second Year of Service:

1. Phase One

   The main focus of the winter training is boxing and should be continued until the participant completes a free-fight of 3 rounds lasting 2 minutes.

   Körperschule must be repeated and improved; games, especially team sports, are still practiced supporting the exercise material. Trail running must be continued like in the first service year.

11. Phase Two

    The athletic and swimming abilities gained in the first service year must be improved. The technique of the training must also be improved.

    The Reichssport-Medall and the certificate of the German Life Saving Corporation (Still exists today as the D.L.R.G.) must be earned.

    Tournaments must be arranged to bring the physical and mental capabilities of the man to their full potential. The handball and football teams must take part in tournaments in their respective battalions and regiments.

Training Review

Personal inspection of the recruits extends to all branches of the Körperschule and the boxing school. Certain strength and skill exercises (e.g. weight throwing, climbing, moving along a rope, tournaments like obstacle relay races, etc.), usually paint a better picture of the capabilities of the recruits than a test of gymnastic training. Improvements in the Körperschule should be noticeable.

During the second year of service emphasis should be placed on boxing. Sparring matches of up to 3 rounds lasting 2 minutes each are required.

Until the end of April, standard tournaments must take place.

Once each summer, the overall performances in athletics and swimming must be checked. Here, tournaments between companies of a battalion or regiment can be helpful.

The non-commissioned officers are to be proficient in all branches of winter training.

Performance Guidelines

Year of Service	1	2
100 Meter Sprint	14.2 Seconds	13.4 Seconds
200 Meter Sprint	32.0 Seconds	30.0 Seconds
400 Meter Sprint	72.0 Seconds	68.0 Seconds
Broad Jump	4.15 Meters	4.75 Meters
High Jump	1.15 Meters	1.35 Meters
Shot Put	6.50 Meters	8.00 Meters
Grenade Throw	35.0 Meters	42.0 Meters
Swimming	100 Minutes	300 Minutes
Free Swimming	2 Minutes 40 Seconds	9 Minutes

Tournaments

In competition the soldier learns to push himself to the mental and physical limit - competition is thus an exquisite builder of will, toughness, and self-discipline. The top performers in each competitive discipline encourage the remainder of the unit to strive for excellence. At these tournaments, only sport that has body-improving value should be shown.

The junior officers and all non-commissioned officers are to participate in official tournaments. It is also desirable that every junior officer take part in extracurricular (non-mandatory) competitive sports.

Tournaments within companies and regiments are to occur annually. Division and corps championships are to be organized by the responsible command center. Championships of the army or Wehrmacht will be ordered by the high command of the army or Wehrmacht. A command center may be tasked with the execution of the championship.

On occasion there may be tournaments in different age groups and years of service to give the less trained and less able a chance at success.

Weapon tournaments don't belong in the area of physical education but in that of military training as they require that the body is already thoroughly trained. The evaluation of the body is to be carried out on the basis of sports performance.

Medical support should be provided and on site during championships.

Tournament Types: Sport tournaments are held as single and team competitions. The tournament guidelines of the German League of the Reich for Physical Exercise are crucial for the sport tournaments.

- One-on-one battles elicit top performance in competitive disciplines. Especially valuable here are combinations of different exercises, e.g. running, jumping, throwing, and swimming.

- Team tournaments promote fellowship and morale and as such should play a big role in sports festivals. Suitable here are company relay races, competitions, tug of war, etc. Further, large scale competitions can be of great propaganda value.

Tournament Training: Soldiers which take part in competitions must be well conditioned to lessen the risk of injury. Each soldier that registers for a competition is responsible for his own preparations. He must be supervised and guided by an experienced officer or a sport sergeant and doctor while training.

Preparations for a tournament only promise success if they build upon a well trained body, full health, and an exemplary way of life. The main rules of this way of life are: Regular sleep of at least 8 hours, homemade food, and abstinence from drugs. Self-Indulgent behavior damages health and strength. Sexual abstinence is not bad for your health.

To avoid overexertion of the participants during preparations, an occasional dispensation of other duties must be accepted.

Massages are especially valuable in training.

Voluntary Sport

Officers should encourage voluntary off-duty sports activities by personal example. Participation in sports favorably directs the natural inclination of youth to fraternize with their peers. The soldier may practice any sport which he desires in his free time.

Top athletes with national importance, those selected by the Commander, should be given support for the betterment of the Reich. They therefore, as far as their duty allows it, are enabled to train and take part in tournaments regarding their special fields after their second year training. The same support should be given to the hand and football teams.

The sportsmanship and sporting activity of a unit may be supported if the soldiers maintain the reputation of their unit on the basis of their sporting abilities, and can be enhanced further by participation with the Army Sports Association.

The Army Sports Association will mainly support the hand and football players of a battalion and organize them into a team. The Association will organize the participation of these teams in tournaments and games for the German Reich League of Physical Exercise. For each presentation to the public, the Army Sports Association must enhance its allure and reputation through the military and sporting behavior of its members. An active leader is vital for the Association to flourish.

Off-duty sport is regarded as service if it was allowed by the responsible advisor. If the soldier would come to harm, it would be regarded as a service injury according to Section 4 of the Army welfare and provision law.

IV. The Exercises

Sport Regulation Contents

- Mandatory exercises required of each soldier
- Exercises which are especially valuable for the further training of officers, non-commissioned officers, and exceptional soldiers. These exercises are added in small print to the individual practice areas without description

The unit commander may in special cases (lack of equipment, swimming opportunity, etc.) omit certain parts of the mandatory exercises (except athletics). The unit commander may also decide to designate specific exercises as mandatory even though they are optional to the standard infantry - this depends on the nature of his unit (e.g. special forces).

A. Körperschule

The basic physical education takes place in the Körperschule - this includes movement games, gymnastics, and exercises with equipment.

Movement games

Simple exercises in the form of running-, pulling-, throwing-, ball-, and party games are the easiest way to make an untrained recruit versatile and flexible. By this, they awaken and encourage the enjoyment of physical activity. Playing games should therefore form the start of the training. Furthermore, the games serve as a balance and relaxation after heavy exercise routines and so should be continued throughout the year.

Unterball

Participants: 2 teams of 6 players, 1 referee

Equipment: 3 Medicine Balls

Setup: Mark a rectangle 16m by 12m, and suspend a rope across it cross-wise at a height of 80cm to create two equally sized zones.

Objective: The goal is to make a ball pass over or touch the opposing team's back line. Any ball that touches the rear of the playing field boundary of the opposite team is considered a point so long as it passed under the rope. A point is also granted to the non-offending team if a ball or player touches the leash, or a ball is thrown over the leash. The winner is the party that scores the highest in 10 minutes.

Rules: An out of bounds ball landing on the sides of the field is not evaluated and must be thrown back into the center of the field by a referee. Teams must stay in their own zones.

Uberball

Participants: 2 teams of 6 men

Equipment: 1 Medicine Ball

Setup: Cordon off a rectangle 10-20m long and 6-12m wide. Divide the rectangle into 2 equal parts with a 2m high line. The teams take position on opposite sides of the line.

Objective: Every time the ball touches the ground on one team's side, the opposite team gets a point.

Points are further scored:

- When the ball touches the line or goes under the line
- When the ball touches the ground outside the playing field (the team whose side it lands on gets one point)
- If the hand of the thrower crosses the line.

Whichever team reaches 20 points first wins.

Rules: The players of each team divide themselves appropriately into front and back players.

The ball is thrown over the line and must always be caught.

The ball must be thrown from wherever it was caught.

Throws that are intercepted before they go out of bounds count as catches.

The lines marking the field count as part of the playing field.

The teams switch sides after 10 points.

Rout

Participants: About a dozen men

Equipment: None

Setup: All players except one are lined up in a row, each clinging to the hips of the man in front. The front man has his arms spread out; opposite of him is the lone player - the attacker.

Objective: The attackers job is to break the row and separate the connection of one or more players while the players in the row must try to prevent this. If the attacker has successfully broken the row, he takes his place as the last person in the row and the player at the front becomes the attacker.

Rules: The front player in the row may block the attacker with outstretched arms without holding him. The players in the back may swing right when the attacker comes from the left and vice versa.

Equestrian

Participants: Any number of equal teams of up to 10 men each

Equipment: None

Setup: The teams are each queued behind a starting line. 20-25m away from the starting line, a finish line is marked in parallel.

Objective: The teams must, in turn, carry their teammates across the finish line. The team whose members all cross the finish line first wins.

Rules: On the command "Go!", the second man in each row jumps on the back of the first and is carried from the start line to the finish line. When they cross the finish line, the man carrying stays at the finish while the carried player runs back to the row and carries the next player in line. This continues until all members of a team have crossed the finish line.

Impact Relay

Participants: Any number of equal teams up to 10 men each

Equipment: 1 Medicine Ball per Team

Setup: The teams line up with 2 meters distance between teammates. The first player in each row is given a ball.

Objective: The first player in the row must throw the medicine ball to each player in his row, each passing it back and then sitting down in turn. The last player in the row runs up and takes the place of the first. The winner is the squad who first returns every player to his starting position.

Rules: On "Go!" the lead player throws the ball to next player in the row, who then throws the ball back and sits down. The first player then throws to the next closest standing player and so on until the last player in the row is thrown the ball - that player then runs with the ball 2 meters in front of the previous lead player and becomes the new lead player, all players stand up.

Obstacle Course

Participants: Any number of teams of up to 10 men each

Equipment: None

Setup: Behind a drawn line, arrange the teams in rows. 25 meters away, opposite and facing the teams, arrange corresponding rows of men separated from each-other by 5 meters. These men will be the obstacles. The obstacles may be modified as fitting. For example, the first kneels, the second stands with legs wide, kneels, the fourth lays down etc.

Objective: Each player from each team must complete the obstacle course. The first team to have all members complete the course wins.

Rules: On "Go!", the first player in each row runs towards the obstacles; per the example, the first is jumped over, the second crawled through, the third jumped over, the fourth ran around. Then the player runs back to his row and tags the next team mate who then completes the course in turn

Medicine Ball Relay

Participants: Any number of equal teams up to 20 men each

Equipment: 1 Medicine ball per team

Setup: Each team stands in aligned in separate rows, with the front player about 3 meters away in a marked location holding the medicine ball.

Objective: The team must work to roll the medicine ball through their legs, the last man bringing up the ball to the front of the line to repeat the process until everyone on the team has returned to their original position. The winner is the squad, who first returns every player to his starting position.

Rules: On the command "Go!", the front player rolls the ball through their legs, and each player in turn tries to accelerate the rolling ball by striking it with their hand.

The last in line receives the ball kneeling and runs past the right side of the squad to replace the first player. During this part each player moves one space back.

If the ball exits the squad before reaching the last player the game restarts from where the ball left the squad.

Handball

Participants: 2 teams of 6 players each - 3 strikers, 1 runner and 2 defenders per team

Equipment: A handball, rugby, or medicine ball

Setup: Arrange a field 30m by 15m with a team on each side. Gravel or hard frozen ground is not suitable as a playing surface. The goals are 4m wide and centered 3m in front of the lower boundary lines of the playing field.

Objective: Pass the ball though the opponent's goal line while avoiding them doing the same. The team with the most points at the close of play wins.

Rules: At the start of the game and after each goal, each team stands on their goal line. The ball is thrown into the middle of the field at the whistle.

The ball may be thrown and pushed with the hands or carried any amount of steps. The ball can be played behind the goal, but a goal can only be set from the front.

The ball can be taken out of the opponent's hand. The owner of the ball may be held below the arms by the opponent as long as he holds the ball - an opponent held in this way must play the ball within 5 seconds.

A free-throw is imposed if:

· The ball is intentionally pushed or kicked by foot

· The opponent is held incorrectly

· A player does not play the ball within 5 seconds of being held

· Unnecessarily rough or dangerous play occurs

If the ball exceeds the playing field boundaries, the ball is brought back into the field by a throw from a player of the non-fouling team.

If two players make an error at the same time, the referee throws the ball in.

The duration of the game can be set as desired, though it is recommended to play 2 halves of 10 minutes each.

Volksball

Participants: Two equally strong teams, each up to 20 players.

Equipment: 1 or more Handballs

Setup: Mark a rectangle 20m by 10m, divided into two equally sized zone by a cross-wise center line. Both teams face each other across the center-line. One player from each side is positioned behind the opposing teams zone

Objective: The goal of the game is to eliminate opposing players by striking them with a ball. The winning team is the one that first depletes the other team's ranks.

Rules: At the start of the game, the ball is thrown up by the referee on the middle line. The party that catches the ball immediately starts the game.

The two players positioned behind the enemy zones cannot be eliminated, but may eliminate opposing players by throwing the ball from outside the boundaries of the zone. For all other players, players may only be eliminated by throwing the ball from within the bounds of the zone.

Players are not eliminated if they catch the ball.

Every person hit must leave the field. Eliminated players may then surround the opponent's zone boundary and pass the ball back to their teammates still in play - however they cannot eliminate players.

The game becomes more difficult when playing with 2 balls, or when it is allowed to catch the ball or to fend off the ball by smacking it away by hand.

Assorted Games

Examples of other games: flying ball, hunter ball, neck ball, tug of war games over a line or from a circle as a competition, etc.

Gymnastics Without Equipment

The gymnastics practitioner should methodically loosen, stretch, and strengthen the muscles, which thereby prepares the body for athletic performance.

The starting positions for the Easing, Stretching, and Strengthening exercises are as follows:

Resting (Fig. 1)

Square (Fig. 2)

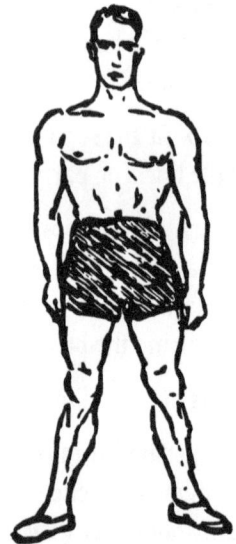

Straight (Fig. 3)

Fig. 1

Fig. 2

Fig. 3

Step (Fig. 4)

Fig. 4

Kneeling (Fig. 6)

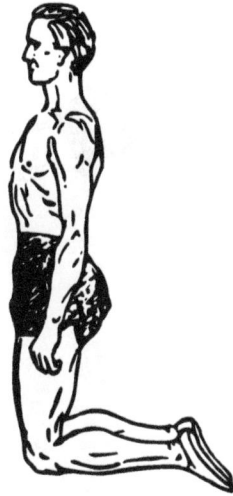

Fig. 6

Sitting (Fig. 5)

Fig. 5

Push Up position (Fig. 7)

Fig. 7

Abdominal (Fig. 8)

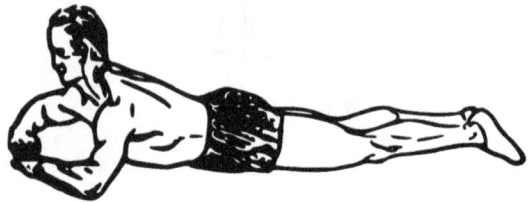

Fig. 8

Prone (Fig. 9).

Fig. 9

Assembly

On command, the soldiers will separate into ranks, 3 meters distance from one another on the left and right, and 2 meters distance from one another in the front and back. Every soldier is to assume the resting position (Fig. 1).

The Practice of Gymnastics

Practice is to be alternated between Arm, Torso, and Leg exercises. The exercise group begins with Warm-Up exercises, followed by Stretching and Strengthening exercises.

After several strenuous exercises, an Easing exercise follows appropriately. Gymnastics without equipment should not last longer than 15 minutes.

The exercises are announced and presented. If the exercise is known, the presentation and lesson can be omitted. Each exercise starts and ends on the command "Start" or "Stop" in the rest position.

During exercises in the Sitting, Kneeling position, Push-Up, Abdominal and Prone positions, the resting position is taken after the command "stand up". Other suitable exercises can be carried out on the commander's order.

Warm-Up

Jumping Jacks (Fig. 10, 11): From Straight position, jump keeping the arms and shoulders loose. While in the air, the arms are loosely swung out from the sides of the body to above the head, and then back down to the sides of the body. While in the air, alternate from Straight position to Square position and vice-versa on the next jump.

Fig. 10

Fig. 11

Leg Swings (Fig. 12): From Step position, the leg is swung backwards and forwards. The knee and ankle of the swinging leg must be kept loose.

Fig. 12

One-Arm Windmills (Fig. 13): From Square position holding up one arm, circle first one arm and then the other closely to the body forwards then backwards. The torso must not be turned when the arms are circled.

Fig. 13

Torso Circles (Fig. 14): From Square position rotate the torso from the hip by bending, first clockwise then counterclockwise.

Fig. 14

Full Windmills (Fig 15): From Square position, with arms held high, circle both forward then backwards.

Fig. 15

Leg Arcs (Fig. 16): From Step position, the leg is swung forward and sideways in a wide arc back to the starting position. The stationary foot raises to balance on the toe at the height of the arc, and goes back to flat as the other foot lands.

Fig. 16

Hip Bends (Fig. 17): From Straight position, bend the torso forward while simultaneously swinging the arms back and partially bending the knees. Reverse the movement as you return to Straight position.

Fig. 17

Dabs (fig. 18): From straight position, the torso is alternately swung to the left and right, with the respective arm extended, and the other loosely swung to the chest. The hips power the rotation.

Fig. 18

IV

Stretching

Wide Front Stretch (fig. 19): From a wide Straight position, the torso is bent forward far enough for both hands to touch the ground.

The same exercise can be performed with one hand at a time, or extended by swinging the hands down from the upright position through the legs.

Fig. 19

Back Stretch (fig. 20): From Straight position, bend the body backwards by curving the spine and sliding the knees and hips forward. The feet remain flat on the ground and the arms hang loosely at the side.

Fig. 20

Side Stretch (fig. 21): With legs wide and arms raised, the torso is alternately swung to the left and right.

Fig. 21

Falling Deep Squat (fig. 22): From the Straight position, bend the knees quickly and curve the back over them at the lowest point. The arms are extended in front of the body, the neck curves with the back, and the soles of the feet are flat.

Fig. 22

Side Kicks (fig. 23): From Straight position, one leg is swung sideways while the other is planted on the ball of the foot. The arms are spread out to the sides for balance. Alternate legs.

Fig. 23

High Kicks (Fig. 24): From Step position, the rear leg is swung as high forwards and upwards as possible while the standing leg is balanced on the ball of the foot. Alternate legs.

Fig. 24

Back Kicks (Fig. 25): From step position, balance the standing leg on the ball of the foot and swing the thigh sharply backward keeping the knee and ankle joints loose. The arms are swung freely.

Fig. 25

Side Split (Fig. 26): Spread the legs to the sides as far as possible without injury. The exercise should not be performed on slippery ground.

Fig. 26

Squat Stretch (Fig. 27): From a crouch, bend at the waist and touch the ground in front of the toes. With the hands still in contact with the ground, straighten the legs.

Fig. 27

Kneeling Back Stretch (Fig. 28): While kneeling with the knees half a hands width apart and the torso straight, bend the spine back quickly while raising the hips. The arms remain loose at the sides.

Fig. 28

Kneeling Side Stretch (Fig. 29): While kneeling, one leg is extended sideways. The torso is then bent towards the outstretched foot with both arms held up.

Fig. 29

Front Split (Fig. 30): Spread the legs to the front and rear as far as possible without injury. Alternate legs. The exercise should not be performed on slippery ground.

Fig. 30

Forward Toe Touch (Fig. 31): While sitting, put the knees together, fully extend the legs, then touch the toes with both hands simultaneously.

Fig. 31

High T Pose (Fig. 32): The arms are stretched backwards and upwards with the chest pushed out. The heels are lifted when the arms swing back and lowered when the arms swing low. After the zenith of the stretch the heels are lowered, and the arms are lowered and loosely crossed in front of the chest.

Fig. 32

Torso Lift (Fig. 33): From the Prone position with arms to the sides, raise the torso as high as possible, extending the arms as a counterweight. The feet should remain touching the ground.

Fig. 33

Melting Heart Pose (Fig. 34): From the Kneeling position, slide the arms forward while lovering the torso and keeping the thighs straight so that the torso is supported by the extended arms. The spine curves backward as the torso lowers.

Fig. 34

Crossed Toe Touch (Fig. 35): While seated with the legs spread wide, reach out with each hand in turn to touch the opposite foot.

Fig. 35

Dives (Fig. 36): From prone position, lock hands behind the back and raise the torso and legs as high as possible.

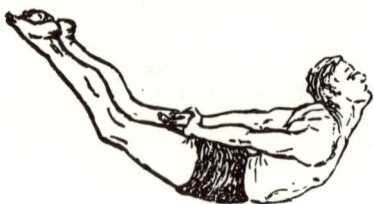

Fig. 36

Partnered Core Stretch (Fig. 37): While seated with legs wide and feet touching, each partner pulls the other in turn. This must be done deliberately and responsively to prevent injury.

Fig. 37

Strength Exercises

Mountain Climbers (Fig. 38): The legs are alternately extended and contracted from a push-up position to a squat position. This can be done with both legs moving in unison, or alternating.

Fig. 38

Double Leg Circles (Fig. 39): While lying on the back, extend the arms to the sides for support and raise the legs. Press the legs together and alternate circle them left and right.

The circling can be executed with closed legs or by continually straddling, sinking, or scissoring the legs.

Fig. 39

Double Toe Touch (Fig. 40): From Prone position, press the legs together, then raise the torso and extend the arms to touch the toes.

Fig. 40

Long Crunch (Fig. 41): From a prone position, a partner holds the legs of the practitioner who extends the arms above their head and bends their torso vertical keeping the arms and spine in line.

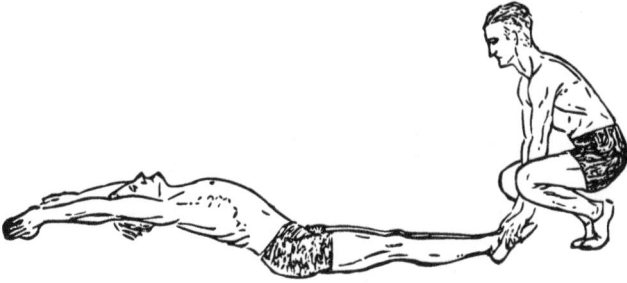

Fig. 41

Push-ups (Fig. 42): The extension is performed quickly and the contraction is performed slowly.

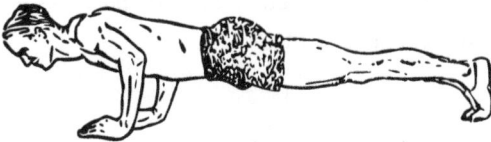

Fig. 42

Partnered One-Legged Squats (Fig. 43): Two practitioners, grabbing each other's hands for balance, simultaneously perform a deep one-legged squat - one with the left leg and one with the right, and then alternate.

When bending the left leg, the right one is pushed forward and vice versa.

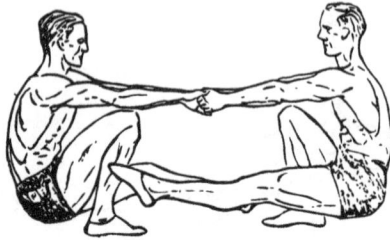

Fig. 43

Partnered Leg Circles (Fig. 44): The two partners sit opposite to each other, one has his legs closed and the other has his opened. The closed legs are higher than the open legs. The man with the closed legs opens and then lowers them as the man with the open legs raises and then opens them, forming a circuit. At no point should either mans legs touch the ground.

The exercise can also be performed with both partners keeping their legs closed and circling them around the other.

Fig. 44

Tuck Jumps (Fig. 45)

Fig. 45

Star Jumps (fig. 46)

Fig. 46

Curve Jumps (fig. 47)

Fig. 47

Movement Exercises

Purpose and Method: Walking, running, and jumping exercises mobilize and warm up the musculature. These movements are especially useful at the beginning of the exercise session, early morning exercise, or sessions in cool and wet weather. Around 20-30 repetitions are performed, each every three steps, while moving in a circle.

1. Walking and running in turns

2. Long, springing strides, similar to skipping (Fig. 48)

3. Running in turns with high jumps (Fig. 49)

After every 3 running steps, jump from the left or right foot alternately.

Fig. 48

Fig. 49

Power Walking (Fig. 50): When power walking, the forward leg is almost fully extended and should contact first with the heel and roll towards the toes along the outer edge of the foot. The arms and shoulders swing vigorously as with running. Each goes as fast as he can.

Speed walking can be performed in turns with walking and running, and can even be carried out as a competition.

Fig. 50

Fig. 51

High Kick Walk (fig. 51): Every third step the leg is swung up towards the head as far as possible. The arms stretch outwards while the torso bends forward. The standing leg rests on the ball of the foot.

Lunges (Fig. 52): During long, deep lunges, the heels are lifted, the torso held erect.

Fig. 52

High Knees and Calf-Kicks : During High Knees, the knees are lifted vigorously, during Calf-kicks the lower leg is loosely raised up rearwards to slap against the calf.

Exercises with Equipment

Gymnastics with equipment is comprised mainly of strength building exercises where the equipment provides the resistance necessary for muscle growth.

Exercises with round weights and barbells or dumbbells are performed slowly.

Medicine ball exercises and throwing exercises with throwing weights are especially valuable for building explosive strength.

Safety Measures: The practitioners must have a workout leader. The leader must ensure sufficient distance between the exercisers.

Medicine Ball

These excercises require two practitioners working in tandem - one to throw and the other to catch, switching after each set.

The medicine ball is caught at chest level by reaching outwards towards the other practitioner who throws the ball.

High Throw (Fig. 53): When throwing, the spine is bent slightly backwards, the ball is swung into a high overhead position, then thrown forward in a high arc with the spine straightened and torso upright.

Fig. 53

Deep Throw (Fig. 54): From the starting position of the high throw, the ball is propelled forward with the core by rapidly bending the torso.

Fig. 54

High Reverse Throw (Fig. 55): With knees initially bent, the ball is swung on an upward arc from under the hips, then thrown backwards over the head by straightening the whole body and planting the bodies weight into the toes.

Fig. 55

Low Reverse Throw (Fig. 56): From the starting position of the High Throw, the ball is accelerated in a downward arc through the legs with the knees slightly bent.

Fig. 56

Fig. 57

Shot Throw (Fig. 57): Balancing the ball in the palm, throw by punching the loaded arm forward and recoiling the other; using the arms, hips and shoulders for power. The ball is pushed at shoulder height from the practitioner to the co-practitioner.

The effect of the exercise can be increased by increasing the speed and force of the throw.

The exercise can also be performed as a long-range throw by taking the same starting position as in the shot put.

Sling Throw (Fig. 58):

Fig. 58

Variations: The High Throw, Deep Throw and Shot Throw can also be exercised while sitting.

Kettle Bell

Front Swing (Fig. 59): The kettle bell is first swung in a high arc with outstretched arms. After the kettle bell reaches its zenith, it is then swung through the open legs with the body absorbing the swings inertia into a squatting position.

The exercise can be performed with only one arm holding the kettle bell, alternating left and right each swing. (Fig. 60).

Fig. 59

Fig. 60

Fig. 61

Side Swing (Fig. 61): From a low starting position, the kettle bell is swung to the side of the torso in a high arc terminating above the head, the kettle bell is then brought back down in an identical arc in controlled fashion.

Circle Swing (Fig. 62): From a high starting position to the side of the torso, the kettle bell is swung one-handed in front of the body to an equally high position on the other side of the body, alternately switching from the left to right hand as it reaches the midpoint of its arc.

Fig. 62

Fig. 63

Halos (Fig. 63): Holding the kettle bell with both arms above the head, the kettle bell is swung alternately left and right around the head in a circling pattern. Over the head the arms are bent slightly, in front of the body they are straight.

Kettle Bell Clean (Fig. 64): The Kettle bell is first swung through the practitioner's bent legs, and accelerated in an upwards arc - at the end of the upwards movement, let go of the kettle bell and catch it with an open hand over the shoulder, bending your arms and knees.

Fig. 65

Fig. 64

Kettle Bell Flip (Fig. 65): Starting with the kettle bell between bent legs, swing it upwards with one arm through the legs, let go of the kettle bell during its upward motion, catching it with the opposite arm after it does a full turn - returning to the starting position as the weight falls.

Throwing Hammer

These exercises are generally used for competitions.

Here it is highly important to have a cleared throwing range and to leave enough space between practitioners.

Starting Position: All throwing hammer exercises begin from this position. The practitioner squats in front of the weight on the ground so that he can grab the weight with an overhand grip and straight arms (Fig. 66).

Front Throw (Fig. 67): The mechanics of this exercise are the same as those for the upwards portion of the kettle bell Front Swing except the hammer is released at the zenith to fly in a arc out from the front of the body.

High Reverse Throw (Fig. 68): Uses the same mechanics as the medicine ball High Reverse Throw.

Fig. 66   Fig. 67   Fig. 68

Halos (Fig. 69): Uses similar mechanics to kettle bell Halos.

Out of the starting position the weight will be swung backwards through the opened legs to build momentum, then forward, up and to the right and circled left around the head.

The weight will be swung deep behind the back on the right then high in the front left. The arms are in a straight position when in front of the body, and bent when behind the head.

Halo Throw (Fig. 70.): After circling the weight once or twice, the weight is to be thrown sideways with straight arms over the left shoulder

Fig. 69   Fig. 70

Barbell

While exercising, have a spotter to prevent the barbell falling backwards.

1. Clean with one arm and both arms (Fig. 71).

2. Jerk with one arm and both arms (Fig. 72).

Fig. 71

Fig. 72

Shot Put

Using a 5 or 7 ¼ kg shot, throw it straight up and alternate hands with each catch.

Exercises on Gymnastic Equipment

Gymnastic equipment training is to be used to strengthen the body, training to overcome obstacles and rough terrain. Perfect form is not required.

Safety precautions: To prevent accidents, supervision and assistance is strictly required. This is primarily necessary when doing jumps over gymnastic equipment or dismounting from the horizontal and parallel bar. In the beginning assistance is provided by the teacher, and later by others instructed in the exercise.

Dismounts are to be cushioned with a mat or deep raked sand pit.

Bar

Pull Up: It is advised to train with both underhand and reverse grip. The chin must go above the bar.

High-bar Swing: From a standing position, grab the bar with both hands and swing back and forth on the bar by shifting the legs back and forth and using the upper body. Build up momentum to swing fully over the bar.

Squat: Grabbing the bar with both arms set wide, simultaneously push-off with the lower body and pull with the upper body while contracting the legs to land on top of the bar with both feet.

High-bar Rotations (Fig. 73): Starting from a swing, bring yourself above the bar so that your feet are above your head, changing the position of one hand to and Eagle grip. As the swing continues, the hand that is in the eagle grip stays on the bar while the other hand is lifted off the bar and the torso fully rotates. The other hand reconnects with the bar once the torso rotation has finished and before the body completes the swing downward. Switch hands with each rotation.

Fig. 73

Fig. 74

Muscle-up (Fig. 74): As you reach the top of a standard pull-up, rotate one arm above the bar and use it to push your shoulders up above the bar bringing in your second arm to do the same, ending with both arms fully extended above the bar.

Parallel bars

Dips (Fig. 75)

Climb Over (Fig. 76): Starting with the same mechanics as the Bar Squat, mount the first bar then climb over and dismount from the second.

Vault (Fig. 77): From a run up, vault of the parallel bars by placing a hand on each bar and swinging over

Fig. 76

Fig. 75

Fig. 77

Uneven Bars

Vault-Over (Fig. 78): Starting with the same mechanics as the Bar Squat, mount the lower bar then vault over the high bar.

Climb-Over (Fig. 79a, b, c): Starting with the same mechanics as the Bar Squat, climb over the low bar first, then the higher bar, then dismount and do the exercise in reverse.

Fig. 78

Fig. 79c

Fig. 79b

Fig. 79a

Seated Spin (Fig. 80): With one hand on each bar, fully extend the legs and swing them back so the feet are above the head. Allow the legs to fall and use the momentum to swing the legs over the lower bar, the legs remain extended and the whole body rotates around the hand gripping the lower bar with both hands acting as anchors (the hand gripping the upper bar will release and re-grip the upper bar as appropriate to allow the rotation to occur). The rotation completes with the soldier sitting on the lower bar and the legs pointed inward.

Tap Swings (Fig. 81): Hanging on the higher bar, swing underneath it and over the lower bar, arching the back to avoid collision.

Fig. 80

Fig. 81

Vaulting Horse

Vault (Fig. 82): From a run, vault the horse by planting one arm and swinging the body over with the sine and legs straightened.

Squat (Fig. 83): Placing the arms wide on the horse, squat down then simultaneously push off with the lower and upper body, then contract the legs to land on top of the horse with both feet.

Squat Vault (Fig. 84): Using similar mechanics to the squat, push off more strongly to vault over the horse in a squat position.

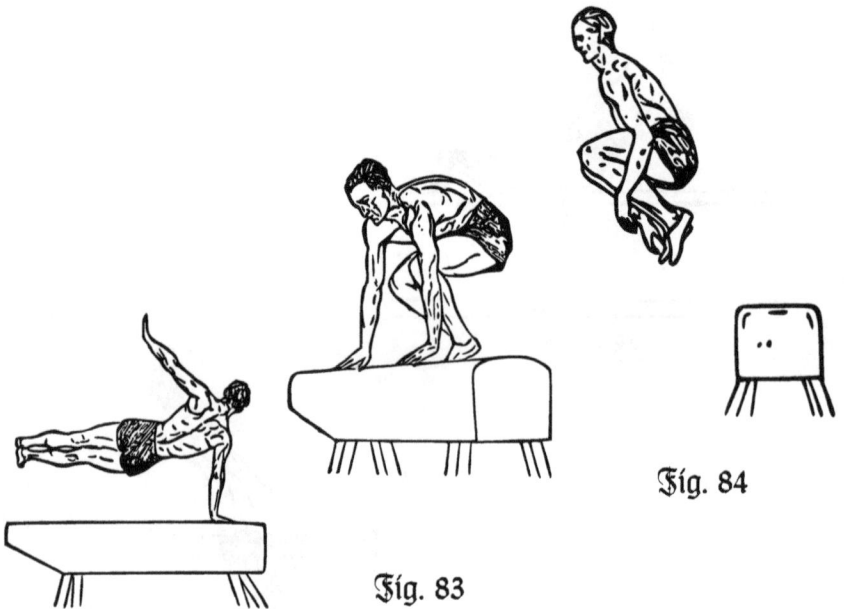

Fig. 84

Fig. 83

Fig. 82

Plant (Fig. 85): Using whatever style preferred, leap onto the horse

Free Jump (Fig. 86): Using whatever style preferred, leap over the horse.

Running Vault (Fig. 87): With arms down to the sides, put one foot on top of the back of the horse, lift yourself up and run across it. Dismount from the horse in a squatting position

Straddle Vault: Approaching the horse from the back at a run, Leap with the shoulders forward, plant both hands on the back of the horse and push off as the legs come forward - vaulting over the horse and landing on the feet.

Fig. 85

Fig. 86

Fig. 87

Rope

Rope climbs are especially strength-building exercise. When rope climbing, make sure to grip the rope with both feet and legs. Climbs can also be performed with a double rope.

Obstacle Courses

By the appropriate assembly of gymnastic equipment and the issuing of instructions, obstacle courses are set up to be overcome as quickly as possible in competition. They are skipped, overtaken, undertaken and exceeded as fitting. In particularly difficult exercises, helpful-orders must be given.

Example Course:

- Climbing and vaulting a waist-high bar or horse

- Jumping over the horse, squatting on or standing on the horse, running over the back of the horse and jumping over a presented obstacle such as jumping a hurdle, a bar, or a higher horse

- Climbing and jumping from one bar to another of unequal height, squatting on one horse and jumping over to another while overcoming obstacles

- Vault over a horse, turn around and back-flip

- Crawl under a bench or other obstacles, free jump over a perpendicularly crossed horse and climb or hang onto a rope

Floor Exercises

Floor exercises make the body supple and flexible. These exercises should only be done on soft surfaces. Difficult ground exercises, such as forward somersaults and flips (saltos), may only be carried out by people who have the necessary physical preparation and ability.

Forward Roll: Example Exercises:

- Rolling forward from the approach and start-up (Fig. 88)

- Forward roll several times in a row

- Jumping and then rolling forward into a handstand

- Handstand and then handstand with subsequent roll forward

Fig. 88

Backward Roll: Example Exercises:

- Roll backwards from the seated position to the kneel position (Fig. 89a)
- Roll backwards from the squatted kneel position to a handstand (Fig. 89b)
- Roll backwards from the handstand to a standing position (Fig. 89c)
- Roll backwards with closed and squatted legs
- Roll backwards into a handstand

Fig. 89a

Fig. 89b

Fig. 89c

Pike Roll (Fig. 90): An assistant may help the practitioner by pushing them through portions of the roll if they are getting stuck.

Fig. 90

Example Exercises:

- Pike roll from atop exercise equipment (jumping with both feet)
- Pike roll from a running start (jump with both feet)
- Pike roll over 1 to 3 adjacent people (laying flat)
- Pike roll over 1 to 3 side by side people (benches)

Assorted Floor Exercises: Handstand (performed with help from an assistant), Cart-Wheel, Front Flip

Stall Bars

Torso Bends: With back to the stall bars, grabbing the rung at hip height, bend the torso forward and then recoil.

Stall Squat: With back to the stall bars, keeping the feet wide, grab the rung at hip height, squat deeply.

Hanging Leg Swings: Either facing towards or away from the wall, hang from an upper rung so that the feet are off the ground, swing the legs from the hip alternately left and right.

Stand-ups: Sitting, facing the wall with open or closed legs, reach forward, grab a rung, and bend the knees as the body is pulled into a squat position.

Side Splits: Face the rack and grab the bars at shoulder height, spread the legs open and lower yourself down into a split.

Front Splits: Facing away from the rack, grab the bars at hip height, keep one leg in place while sliding the other forward, lowering yourself into a split.

Hanging Leg Raises: With back to the wall, hang with the feet off the ground, raise and lower the legs in unison.

Standing Side Splits: Stand facing the stall bars, grip the bar at chest height. Keeping one leg planted, bend sideways at the waist and raise the leg out on the opposite side until it is horizontal, then spring back to the standing position. As flexibility improves, raise leg higher until approaches vertical. This exercise can be performed with the leg bent or extended for added resistance.

Dips: Standing with your back against the stall bars, bend forwards at the waist and grab the second bar from the floor. Slide your legs forward and keep them straight. Bend your arms at the elbow to perform a dip and then straighten them back up

Incline Arm Ups: In a wide push-up position, place both hands on the third rung from the bottom. Keeping one arm straight, bend the other arm, then straighten it, alternating arms with each repetition. This exercise can be made more or less difficult by using a lower or higher rung.

B. Athletics

Through the exercises of athletics, the soldier learns to perform the natural movements of running, jumping, and throwing in a practical and energy-saving manner, thereby increasing his performance in all areas of military service. The aim is to provide a wide range of training, ideally augmented by voluntary exercises.

Through competitions and performance measurements, the ambition of the soldier is to be promoted in a healthy way and his voluntary commitment fostered until forces are deployed.

The Run

The run is the most valuable exercise. Through running, stamina and speed are acquired and the internal organs are stimulated and developed.

A loose and buoyant movement is to be sought and any unnecessary tension or cramping of the muscles avoided. Particular attention must be paid to ensure full forward swinging of the legs (Fig. 91). The faster the run, the more the upper body pushes forward, and the stronger the legs are stretched during repulsion and the stronger the arms swing (Fig. 92). With slow running, the torso is upright, arms and legs swing lightly and loosely. The feet point in the direction of travel.

Fig. 91

Fig. 92

In a sprint, the foot springs up, with medium-fast and slow running the foot is placed with the whole sole forward and rolled off.

Breathing takes place through the mouth and nose. Thorough exhalation must be ensured.

Practice: The correct running style is acquired through the following running exercises:

1. Unforced running at a slow pace on the track (each level course is suitable)

2. Run with short, loose steps dribbling a ball with the feet (football/soccer run) to achieve the required looseness of the leg and arm work

3. Increasing runs over 100 to 400 meters to train in each running style. The speed of the run is gradually increased during training

4. Runs with tempo changes: The runner changes speed repeatedly, initially from medium speed, then to a slow speed, then to an all-out run at full speed, and then back into the initial pace

Cross-Country

Cross-country running is the best endurance training. The soldier learns to adapt his running style to difficult terrain.

The training of endurance depends on the length of the track and the pace. Shorter runs (2-3km) at a lively pace train endurance as well as longer runs (up to 10km) at a slow pace.

The training begins with slow runs in light terrain (solid ground) over 2-3km, which are interrupted in the beginning with breaks between stages in training. The length of the track, the speed of the run, and the difficulties of the terrain are gradually increased.

The Sprint

The sprint is carried out over distances of 100, 200, and 400m (short distance run). Starting practices, wind sprints, and tempo changes are necessary to achieve greater performance in the short distance run.

Repeated short runs over 60 to 100m, occasionally over 200 to 300m, and, for the particularly rugged given the necessary endurance to be able to pass this route at a fast pace, the 400m, 500m or 600m track run

Every short-distance runner should also be trained in the start and relay change. The usual relays are 4 by 100m and 4 by 400m

The Start: Starting holes are carefully and deeply dug with firm back walls. The non-dominant foot is placed on the starting line with the dominate foot behind it, bend the knee of the dominant leg down near the ankle of the forward foot, the tip of the foot

On the command "On your marks" the runner puts his feet in the starting holes, kneels down, puts his hands on the starting line supporting the body, arms straight roughly shoulder width apart, fingers touching the ground with the palms pointed inwards (Fig. 93).

Fig. 93

On the command "Get set" the runner lifts the knee of the dominant posterior leg from the ground so bend of the leg forms an angle of more than 90°, pushes the upper body forward, transfers the body weight to the stretched arms and breathes deeply.

The view is slanted forward to the ground (Fig. 94). On the run-off command "Go" (and/or a pistol shot) the runner pushes himself with both feet out of the starting holes.

The first steps are short, fast, and loose, the arms swing sharply angled as the legs. The runner gradually straightens up to a natural running posture. After the start, 20 to 30m must always be sprinted through.

Practice:

1. Practice the individual positions

2. Easy starts, ensure that the arm work is correct from the first step

3. Sprint over 20 to 30m at full speed

4. Pre-set starts and runs (worse runners get a target) up to 60m They are often used as an incentive for unmotivated runners

Fig. 94

Fig. 95

Baton Pass

Passing the baton is the technical prerequisite for the team effort in short distance running.

The runner receiving the baton stands at the beginning of the 20m transfer spot and awaits the runner approaching at the fastest pace with the rod in his left hand.

As soon as he has reached a mark designated 6-8m before the beginning of the transition location (the distance depends on the speed of both runners), the receiver goes off at full speed with full arm motion.

Shortly before the next runner has given the baton, he stretches out the right arm to the back (hand spread out stretching from the body), the bringer simultaneously pushes the baton rod from under into the hand of the receiver with the front extended left arm (Fig. 95). The receiver immediately takes the baton into his left hand.

Practice:

1. Relay change while walking, then slow and fast running

2. Relay change in the 20m location with auxiliary stamp determination.

3. In order to determine the auxiliary marks safely, it is necessary to pass through the full distance in the competition order of the stops.

4. Practice competitions in different seasons.

Fig. 95

Assorted Runs

Other running distances are: medium distances over 800m, 1000m, 1500m.
Long-distance runs over 3000m, 5000m, 10,000m, 25km, 42.2km (Marathon).
Hurdles over 100m, 200m, 400m Steeplechase (obstacle course run) over
3000m.

The Jump

The jump takes the form of a stride leap, high jump, or long jump.

The Stride Leap (Fig. 96): The stride leap is executed on the run over
low obstacles which are up to 90cm high and should not hinder any running
movement. The runner lands on his swinging leg and immediately continues
running.

The push-off leg trails behind just like when running. At obstacles which are
over 70cm high, it is trailed laterally.

The High Jump: The high jump is executed as either a Tuck jump or
Scottish jump.

Tuck Jump (Fig. 97): The Tuck jump is started by running forward,
both legs tucked to the body while jumping, and ended by landing on
both feet.

Fig. 96

Fig. 97

Scottish Jump (Fig. 98): The Scottish jump is performed by running from the side, so that the swinging leg is facing the bar.

The legs are swung over one after another; the jumper lands on the swinging leg.

The run-up to the high jump is a moderate run in which the last three to four steps are performed powerfully.

The Long Jump: The long jump is a tuck jump in which the lower legs are swung forward for landing.

To avoid falling back the jumper swings his arms forward and pushes his knees forward when he lands (Fig. 99, Fig. 100).

Fig. 100

Fig. 99

Fig. 98

The run-up to the long jump is an uphill run in which the maximum speed must be reached several steps before jumping off. The speed of the run-up and height of the jump determine the distance.

Predisposed jumpers may use the same style for the high- and long- jump, if appropriate.

Practice:

1. Jumps from the standing position to strengthen the bounce and to learn the necessary stretch when jumping.

    I. Long jump from the standing position.

    II. Triple jumps from different standing positions (on both legs, on one leg, stride leap, sporty triple jump, hop, step, jump).

    III. High jump from the standing position as tuck jump.

2. Jumps with a light run-up.

    I. Jump with both legs, high- and long- jumps.

    II. Jump with the takeoff leg and relaxed but high long jumps.

3. Long- and wide- jumps with run-up.

4. In cross-country runs, jumps over ditches, hedges, in sand pits, etc. are performed.

Assorted Jumping Exercises: Long jump as running jump (including correct run-up technique), High jumps in various techniques (including roll-overs), Pole vault, Triple jump with run-up.

The Throw

It is prohibited for the exercising person to return training equipment by throwing it back. The front and sides of the throwing field are to be kept free of personnel.

The Hand Grenade Throw

The hand grenade throw is practiced for both distance and aim.

Standing Position: The hand grenade is held firmly but not too tightly in the throwing hand. The body weight rests on the right leg, the upper body is slightly bent forward. The throwing arm is stretched almost fully backward (Fig. 101).

When throwing, the left leg is lifted off the ground first as the body leans away from the throwing direction. As the body begins the throw, the left leg returns to the ground as the body pivots forwards, the right leg pushes and stretches as the throw nears completion, the right hip and shoulder are thrown forward and the throwing arm abruptly snaapped forward past the right side of the head (Fig. 102).

Fig. 101   Fig. 102

Run-Up: The run-up is from a distance about 15-20m. It is an accelerating run, in which the last 2 to 4 steps are carried out so that the right leg is placed over the left (cross step) and the thrower thus enters the throwing position.

At the run-up, the hand grenade is carried in front of the body.

In order to avoid shoulder and elbow injuries, only light throws are required in the beginning, and performance throws later.

Practice:

1. Light throws from the standing position to learn how arm and body work in conjunction

2. Throw from slow run-up, practicing the cross step

3. Throw from moderate run-up, practicing the cross step

4. Throw from fast run-up, defining a mark at the beginning of the cross step

5. Hand grenade target throws

The Shot Put: The thrower stands with his left side to the throwing direction. The shot lies at the base of the fingers with the thumb spread out. The right leg is bent, the upper body slightly bent away from the throwing firection, the shot rests on the right shoulder (Fig.103).

When thrown, the left leg raises and lowers a little to the left of the throwing direction on the front edge of the circled floor.

The push is done by strongly extending the right leg, advancing the whole right throwing side over the stretched, stiff left leg (Fig. 104), and straight pushing of the throwing arm at an angle of 45 ° over the edge of the circled floor (Fig. 105).

The right leg must not lose contact with the ground until the ball has released the hand.

Practice: Practicing of partial movements is to be avoided.

1. Brief practice of the starting position and the process of movement without a shot.

2. Push from the standing position with a 5kg shot.

3. Push from the standing position with a 7.25kg shot.

Fig. 103   Fig. 104   Fig. 105

The Stone Toss

The stone toss requires the same technique as the shot put when standing upright (Fig. 106, Fig. 107). The stone is carried one-handed in front of the chest (Fig. 108). By moving the right leg over the left (cross-step), the thrower moves into the throwing position.

Practice:

1. Push off the starting position

2. Running with the stone and learning the cross-step

3. Push with a full start of 15-20m length right and left

Assorted Throwing Exercises: Shot Put with pitch, Discus throw, Javelin, Hammer throw.

Fig. 106

Fig. 107

Fig. 108

C. Swimming

Supervision and Classification

During swimming lessons, an officer or a non-commissioned officer trained as a swimming instructor is to be designated as the inspector. He is responsible for the practitioners and arranges the necessary safety measures.

Safety Measures: The supervisor and teaching staff must observe the following rules:

- Ear, eye, and skin patients should not swim without medical permission;

- People who have been ill must be specially watched

- People should not go into the water with a full stomach or while overheated

- After great efforts (marching) or little sleep (watch), efforts to swim must be avoided

- Do not use outdoor baths when the water temperature is low for too long

- For continuous swimming, the skin must be greased to reduce the heat loss

The senior officers issue safety regulations according to conditions. In accordance with the general safety regulations, the inspector must arrange the division of troops, assortment to the free-swimming and non-swimmer pool, the change of departments, the classification of the teaching staff and the emergency services (the latter, if necessary, in consultation with the lifeguard). The safety regulations are to be formulated accordingly for indoor swimming pools, if the civilian bath master does not lead the supervision.

Special measures are to be taken when swimming outside the institution. Lifeguards who swim next to the students are to be marked by bright caps. A lifeboat (wide wooden barge) must be present. Canoes and folding boats are not suitable as lifeboats.

For deep and opaque water, it is advisable to secure students who are already swimming without a line with a life vest or diver's respirator. Care should be taken when jumping into water of unknown depth.

In each institution are to be displayed:

- The safety requirements for the institution concerned;
- The panels of D.L.R.G. for resuscitation after drowning.

Non-Swimming Lessons

The goal of this training is to prepare for the breaststroke and backstroke.

Practice: Lessons are given in shallow water without a device. Equipment-free training has the advantage of being natural and many can be trained concurrently. Training enhances the student's sense of security as they are accustomed to water training gradually with patience for physical and mental inhibitions. Dry swimming exercises can be taught quickly. The individual exercises should be done first on land and then in the water.

Water Acclimatization

The pupil must recognize that his body remains afloat without movement of the arms and legs on the surface as soon as the lungs are filled with air. Controlled breathing is the first prerequisite.

Example Acclimatization Exercises:

1. Basic Acclimatization: Standing and walking in shoulder deep water, deep inhaling and exhaling

2. Diving Acclimatization:

   I. Brief immersion of the head underwater, immediate emergence

   II. Inhale, submerge, stay underwater for a few seconds, exhale under water

   III. Submerge, keep the eyes open to look for underwater objects.

3. Buoyancy Acclimatization:

   I. Fill the lungs with air, draw in the arms and legs to form a ball. Exhale to sink then quickly resurface. This is first performed with help then without as the soldiers acclimatizes

   II. Floating, stretch the body in breast and back position with assistance

   III. Drifting in an extended breast stroke and back position, first with another student pulling, then with another student pushing off the bottom or edge of the pelvis

Breast Stroke

The leg and arm movements are alternated to create continuous forward propulsion.

Leg Movement: To prepare to kick, the legs are bent at the knee with the heel approaching the buttocks, the legs are spread wide, the feet are bent towards the shin.

When kicking against the water, the legs are straightened backwards, the feet are bent away from the shin to maximize leverage. The legs are brought together following an arc as they straighten.

> **Practice**: In shallow water, the hands support the body on the ground or hold it to the edge of the pool.

Arm Movement: To prepare for the arm stroke, the arms are fully extended in front of the head, the hands form a wedge with the tips of the fingers touching and the palms pointed inwards.

To begin the stroke, the palms are rotated to point out to either side of the body, the arms remain extended and begin to sweep to either side of the body. When the hands are shoulder width apart, bend the elbows and rotate the palms down for better leverage.

When the hands have pushed down to shoulder height, bring the hands inward and push them forward reforming the wedge to prepare for another stroke.

> **Practice**: In shallow water, the student lies stretched out on the arms of the helper.

Breathing: The practitioner inhales during the arm stroke and exhales during the kick.

Coordination of movement:

1. Inhalation with the arm stroke (Fig.109).

2. Bending the arms and hands under the chest while bending the legs with open knees (Fig. 110).

3. Exhalation while kicking and driving the hands forward (Fig. 111, 112, 113).

Practice: If the student can control the coordination of the movements, he pushes himself off the side of the pool edge, into the swimming pool, and tries to carry out the motion several times.

After each stroke the student must pause and let the body glide forward.

The distance to be covered must be gradually increased.

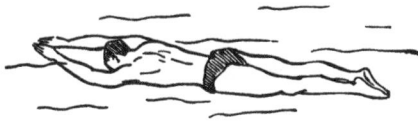

Fig. 109

Fig. 110

Fig. 111

Fig. 112

Fig. 113

Double Backstroke

Lying on the back, the body should be outstretched, and the head should be in the water with water coming up to the ears.

Arm Movement: Extend the arms behind the head so that the hands are close together with the palms pointing outward. With arms extended, the hands are swept to the sides of the body until they touch the thighs.

Leg Movement (Fig. 114): Continuously, the legs are to kick against the water. As the feet kick down the knee bends and the foot is bent towards the shin, as the leg kicks up the leg is extended and the foot is bent away from the shin. While one leg kicks down, the other raises alternating to create propulsion. The leg movement is similar to that required by the breaststroke.

Breathing (Fig. 115): Breathing deeply through their nose and their mouth, the swimmer should breath in as they drive their arms through the water and breath out slowly when their hands touch their hip.

After the movements are performed, the swimmer should lay stretched out in the water in order to float in the water.

It is easier to learn positioning, movements, and breathing in the backstroke than in the breaststroke. This technique will allow the student to become more comfortable in the water.

Fig. 114

Fig. 115

Deep Water

A life-jacket can be used when first transitioning to swimming in deep water. In order to increase safety, the student can swim next to a rope, which would be tied to a pier or boat.

Fig. 116

Later, the student should swim without a rescue rope next to a boat, under the supervision of an experienced swimmer (a lifeguard if possible). At the same time the student should practice jumping (foot-first Pencil jumping, or Cannon Balls Fig. 116) from a rope, from the stairs, from the side of the pool and from a one meter high diving board - jumping from taller diving boards is forbidden before passing the swimming proficiency test.

Swimming Proficiency Test

The following points must be met in the presence of an officer:

- Enter the pool by jumping from 1 meter high, using their jumping-style of choice
- Swim for 15 minutes using the breaststroke
- Swim for 15 minutes using the backstroke
- Swim freestyle for more than 15 minutes without stopping

IV

Free Swimming

The student's confidence with the breaststroke and backstroke will be improved through constant practice (long distance swimming of 100-300 meters), at the same time, speed will be improved.

Students who master other forms of swimming will improve their technique through long distance swimming.

Start and Turn

The start and turn are the prerequisites for every regulated swimming exercise.

Start: Jumping from the side of the pool or a starting block, the feet should be a hands length apart, the toes facing towards the pool side or starting block edge, with the knees, arms, and elbows slightly bent, the head somewhat tilted back, the body should be leaned forwards (Fig. 117).

The position should be taken after the commander says "On your marks!". The swimmers jump when they hear the word "Go", the arms should press forwards.

The swimmer should breath in when they first jump, and they should breath out when they emerge.

After the swimmer hits the water, the swimmer's body should glide stretched out flat in the water. The swimmer's head should be face-down in the water between the arms (Fig. 118).

Fig. 117

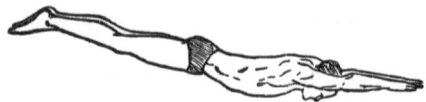

Fig. 118

Turn: Face and grab the bar or side of the pool, the body should be pulled up next to the bar or pool side, but not completely out of the water, breath in before launch (Fig. 119).

Contract the legs to prepare to push off once the grip is released (Fig. 120).

The kick-off should be performed after both of the legs have made contact with the wall (Fig. 121).

The arms should be stretched forward, and the head should be positioned in the water between the arms.

After the kick off from the wall, the swimmer should glide through the water.

Fig. 119

Fig. 121

Fig. 120

Diving

Diving raises the competency of the swimmer, and builds off of the prior swimming exercises. The swimmer's performance should slowly increase; overconfidence, or overzealous diving could lead to injury.

The eyes should be open under water.

Safety Precautions:

Do not dive deeper than 3 meters or swim underwater for a distance greater than 27 meters without the appropriate service certificate.

In the case of opaque water, a floating body (cork, bladder) on the surface must be attached to the swimmer's body with a 5 m long cord (be careful with jetties, rafts and barges).

Deep Diving: Deep diving for objects is carried out by jumping foot- or head-first from the bank, diving board, or swimming position.

Underwater Swimming: Swimming underwater should be performed with the breast-stroke. Buoyancy while in the water should be overcome by swimming at a slightly downward angle. Swimming in a straight line under water can only be improved over time by practice and slowly performing the swimming motions while opening the eyes under water.

The air that was inhaled during the kick-off should be slowly released during the duration of the dive. Before emerging all of the air should be already released.

The most preferable diving-depth is 1.5-2 meters (Do not swim close to bottom of the pool).

Jumping

Safety Precautions: The supervisor should be careful to correctly time the student's jumps to avoid collisions.

Falling, either forwards or backwards off of the platform, into a dive is forbidden due to how common injuries are.

Standing Jump: Jump from a standing position without a walk or run-up. It can be used from a 1-3 meter or 5 meter jumping platform where available.

Cannon Ball: With or without a running start. The legs should be tucked while in the air, the diver should fall feet-first while balled-up into the water. This is best used in unknown or shallow water depths. This type of jump should only be performed from a one meter tall platform.

Running Start: Standing on the back of the board, run at full speed towards the front, jump forward with the body outstretched with the arms thrown forward and the head positioned between the arms (Fig. 122).

The diver should be completely outstretched and at a sharp angle when entering the water, and then straighten out to swim parallel to the bottom of the pool (Fig. 123).

Other jumps from 1-3 meters can be seen on the D.L.R.G's chart of jumping techniques. The most important are the forward dive, the forward and backwards somersaults, the backwards dive, the back flip, and the forwards 1 1/2 flip.

Fig. 122   Fig. 123

Other Swimming Techniques

Hand-Over-Hand Swimming, Doggy-Paddle, Double-Arm Backstroke, Backstroke

Lifeguards

Confident and safe swimmers should aspire to become lifeguards.

A strict standard is to be set for the acceptance of test takers for the German-Life-Rescue society. The test taker must meet the conditions the first time taking the test.

The lifeguards must learn how to swim with clothes on, how to handle someone thrashing in the water, how to rescue someone in the water, resuscitation, and how to behave in stressful situations.

Correspondence between the Wehrmacht and the D.L.R.G. is directly performed by the regiments themselves in abbeys, schools, etc. and the central office of the D.L.R.G. in Berlin.

D. Boxing

Boxing furthers military training by developing the spirit and ability to engage the enemy. Boxing promotes mental and physical well-being, self-confidence, toughness, speed and agility. A soldier trained in boxing is equipped with the mental and physical power necessary to perform well in close combat.

Phase One

The first phase of training involves exercises that can be performed without gloves - these exercises are an important addition to general physical exercise and are to be performed alongside it.

Orthodox Fighting Position

The orthodox fighting position is the starting position for attack and defense. For a right-handed boxer, the right leg is positioned about one step behind and to the right of the left leg, with the left leg resting on the sole, the right resting on the ball with the heel raised, the toes pointing forward, the knees are loose and slightly bent, the weight is evenly distributed on both legs (Fig.124), the upper body is almost upright, and the left shoulder is slightly ahead of the right.

The left arm is bent almost at a right angle. The left hand is raised to the level of the left pectoral. The right arm covers the body, just below the chin (Fig. 125). Both fists are clenched, the thumb rests on the index and middle fingers.

Fig. 124

Fig. 125

Footwork

Quick footwork is the boxer's indispensable means of either attacking or evading the attacker.

The legs are in continuous movement; the legs should not cross, or be too close together.

The following movements are fundamental:

- Advancing/Retreating: When advancing, the front foot advances one step forwards, the back foot follows. When retreating, the back foot retreats one step backwards, the front foot follows.

- Side Step: When side-stepping left, the left foot steps first and the right follows, when stepping right vice-versa.

- Jumping: Both legs perform a small flat jump at the same time. Can move the boxer in any direction.

- Three-Step: The 3-step allows the boxer to cover ground more quickly in any direction e.g. a left-right-left step or a right-left-right step is progressed from one leg to the other with a slight shift of weight.

Practice: A good preliminary exercise for footwork is rope jumping.

- Jump on both legs with a hop in between skips.

- Jump alternately on the left and right leg with a hop in between.

- Jump on both legs without a hop in between.

- Jump alternately on the left and right legs without a hop in between.

All jumps are performed flat with a slight bending of the knee joint. As the skill progresses, the last exercise should be carried out especially. At first, jump only one minute, later up to 3 minutes.

The Straight Punch

Either hand, with power from the shoulder, connects to the target's head or body. The fist hits knuckle first and is turned at the last moment so the back of the hand faces up (Fig. 126). When the punch is completed, the hand returns to guard.

If the straight punch can not be achieved because the opponent is out of reach, the boxer makes a small step with the left foot in order to obtain a favorable distance to the opponent.

Practice: The straight punch is first practiced without footwork, then with step drills, then with variable footwork.

Fig. 126

Defense Against the Straight Punch: Perform the following with a partner (A = Attacker, D = Defender):

- A. attacks with a left straight - D. takes a step back
- A. attacks with a right straight - D. takes a step back
- A. attacks with a left straight - D. takes a step to the right
- A. attacks with a right straight - D. takes a step to the right
- A. attacks with a left straight - D. defends by catching the punch with his right hand (Fig. 127)
- A. attacks with a right straight - D. defends by catching the punch with his right hand
- A. attacks with a left straight - D. defends by redirecting the punch with his right hand (Fig. 128).
- A. attacks with a left straight to the body - D. defends with the back of his right hand.
- A. attacks with a right straight to the body - D. defends with the back of his left hand.

The defense is first practiced from a solid boxing position, then with footwork.

Fig. 127

Fig. 128

The Hook

The hook hits the head or body from the side. When performing the hook, the fist is in the same position as when attempting a straight punch (thumbs up) (Fig. 129).

The arm is more or less bent depending on the distance to the opponent. A wild swing is to be avoided. In the right-hook, the left hand shields the chin.

Practice: The left or right hook is executed like the straight punch, first without sidestep, then practiced with sidestep, then with footwork.

Fig. 129

Defense Against Hooks: These can be defended against by stepping backwards. Perform the following with a partner (A = Attacker, D = Defender):

- A. punches with left hook - D. ducks (Fig. 130).

- For the duck, the head, torso, and legs are slightly bent so that the blow goes overhead. Beware of followup hits.

- A. punches with a right hook - D. ducks.

- A punches with a left hook - D. defends with the back of his right hand, close to his head (Fig. 131).

- A. punches with right hook - D. defends with the back of his left hand.

- A. attacks with a left punch to the body - D. defends with his right hand or forearm (Fig. 132).

- A. attacks with right punch to the body - D. defends with left hand or forearm

Fig. 130

Fig. 131

Fig. 132

The Uppercut

The uppercut is a punch from below. As the uppercut connects the back of the hand is towards the opponent and the arm is bent. The power of the blow is enhanced by vigorously pushing up through the legs. In case of the right hook, the left hand shields.

Practice: The uppercut is practiced like the hook and the straight punch.

Defense Against the Uppercut: These can be defended against with a backward step. Perform the following with a partner (A = Attacker, D = Defender):

- A. punches with a left/right uppercut to the chin - D. defends with open hand (Fig. 133).

- A. punches with a left uppercut to the body - D. defends with the back of his right hand or forearm.

- A. punches with right uppercut to the body - D. defends with the back of his left hand or forearm.

Fig. 133

Double-Strikes

A boxer is more effective if punches are not applied individually, but in quick succession in the form of double-strikes. Double-Strikes are practiced both from a standing position and with footwork:

Double-Strike Examples:

- Left straight to the body, left straight to the head.
- Left hook to the body, left hook to the head.
- Left straight to the head, right straight to the head.
- Left straight to the body, right straight to the head.
- Left hook to the body, right hook to the head.
- Left hook to the head, right hook to the head.
- Left hook to the head, right uppercut to the body.

Shadow Boxing / Mock Battle

The student utilizes everything he has learned in a casual, self-chosen order, with the teacher paying attention to ensure fluid footwork and clean punching technique.

Boxing Equipment

The most important pieces of boxing equipment are wall padding, punching bags, sandbags, platform balls, and speed balls - all of which can be easily made at home.

Using boxing devices, hits and punches are first to be drilled as instructed, then through freestyle shadow boxing.

Phase Two

The second phase of training involves combat. Boxing gloves, weighing 12-14 ounces (340-397 grams), are to always be worn during practice.

Free fighting is only acceptable if attack and defense are mastered. The fight must not transform into a brawl; therefore, a trainer may not oversee more than 3 to 4 fights at a time, so that he can observe all fighters and immediately stop dangerous or unsportsmanlike fighting. In particular, the instructor must make sure that only equally strong opponents fight with each other. All safety measures initiated by the Boxing department must be observed according to competition regulations.

Off-hand Training

The non-dominant left hand is trained in combat through partner exercises.

Off-Hand Fighting: When both contestants can appropriately use the punches learned in attack or defense, free-fighting with the off-hand can begin. The off-handed fight becomes more versatile when the punches are thrown as double punches, while attacker and defender try to land either two straight off-hand punches or off-hand left hooks.

The off-handed fight initially lasts three rounds with one minute each, with growing endurance this increases to three rounds with two minutes each.

Off-Hand Defense: Through Blocking and Countering, the defender avoids or stops a strike by the attacker, either to strike at the same moment or after a short time.

Blocking:

- A. gives a straight left punch to the head - D. catches the punch with his right hand, his left arm moves forward at the same time. A. parries, also.

- A. gives a straight left punch to the head - D. ducks right and at the same time parries on the left side of the attacker. A. parries.

Countering:

- A. gives a straight left punch to the head - D. moves back and counters with a straight punch while moving forward again.

- A. gives a straight left punch (left hook) to the head - D. parries and counters with a left hook to the head or chest. A. parries.

- A. gives a straight left punch (left hook) to the head - D. parries and counters with a left uppercut to the chest.

Training for Free-Fighting

Defending Against Double-Strikes: The straight left and right punches are dodged by moving backwards, left and right hooks and uppercuts are accordingly parried.

In boxing, usually a left punch is followed up with a left punch, and a right punch with a right punch. If the attacker punches left-right, the defendant parries both punches and tries to counter with the right hand, which can be followed by the left.

Practice:

- A. gives a left and right straight punch to the head - D. dodges backwards or to the side, and counters with a right and a left straight punch.

- A. gives a left and right straight punch - D. parries and counters with a straight right punch, which can be followed with a straight left punch.

- A. gives a left and right hook - D. parries and counters both right and left.

- A. gives a left and right hook - D. parries and counters with a right uppercut, which may be followed up with a left hook.

Fighting with Double-Strikes: From this practice the fight with double jabs or punches evolves, while the attacker usually punches left-right and the defender counters right or right-left. In the first practices, the right hand should be used with less force than usual. A fight lasts two rounds with one minute each.

Free-Fighting

Combining off-handed fighting and double-strikes grants the fighter much greater effective reach. The fighter now shouldn't merely apply the examples learned in practice, but find possibilities in the nature of the fight and use them skillfully. He should strive for a certain versatility in his punches. Sometimes it is necessary to disconnect from theory to a degree, since the fight may challenge the fighter in ways the school cannot prepare him for.

As experience in fighting with double punches increases, the fighters will try to land more than two punches. For good fighting, the frequent and adept use of the left hand will be essential.

The second phase of training is completed with a fight over three rounds, each lasting two minutes. The goal of the training is for the practitioner to competently carry out a full fight in the ring to tie theory to practice.

C. Team Sports

As the men grow more powerful, the training of the body is replaced with training that strengthens team work, competitiveness, and fighting spirit. All sports carried out in competitions by the German League of the Reich for Physical Exercise, especially handball and soccer, but also hockey, rugby, basketball, etc., are well suited for enhancing the bodily fitness of the soldier.

Sports teach battle spirit, subordination to the common goal, mental fitness, and individual initiative. Soldiers who have already played in a team before joining the army should, if possible, be supported in their sports. The aim should also be to train all non-commissioned officers and most of the men in the second year of their service in team sports.

The games are to be played by the rules of the German League of the Reich for Physical Exercise.

Handball

Handball is the main sport of the army. It is easier to teach than soccer and doesn't require specialized gear. Each company is to assemble at least one handball or soccer team to play in a yearly regiment competition.

Matches between soldiers and civilians are an important part of public relations between the Wehrmacht and the people.

Drills

Catching and Ball Handling:

- Two-handed catching of chest level, head level, and low balls

- Picking up rolling balls

- Stopping high balls with one hand

- Throwing and catching while moving, in a circle, or while running next to other players

- Left- and right-handed dribbling the ball while moving

- Sidestepping an enemy by turning past, juking, pass-fake, outplaying

- Throwing goals while moving and after catching. Bouncing balls

- Ball and movement training through a team ball game

  - In a small area, two teams of three to five players pass the ball to each other. Each player in possession tries to pass as often as possible. In a competition, each successful pass of a team counts as one point. The first team with 25 points wins

- Position change practice with two wingers and two backs or with two teams without center and circle runner

Throwing:

- One-handed swinging throw below the hip, on shoulder level or above the head
- Two-handed swinging throw below the hip or on shoulder level
- One-handed core or power throw below the hip, on shoulder level or above the head
- Two-handed core or power throw above the head

Tactics

- Explanation of the tasks of each position
- Covering
- Explanation of the flank attack, holding and changing position
- Defending position changes, blocking tactics
- Lineup at first throw, goal throw-off, free throw near the goal, penalty corner throw, long corner throw

Soccer

Drills

Kicks:

- Kick (pass) with the inner side of the foot,
- Kick (pass) with the outer side of the foot,
- Kick with the instep,
- Headers.

Stopping the Ball

- On the ground with the inner side, outer side, sole, calf;
- In the air with the instep, thigh, belly, chest.

Dribbling

- With the inner and outer foot, both left and right.

Tactics

- Zig-Zag passes with two players
- Exercise escaping cover by 2 or 3 players against one, and against parties of equal sizes
- Covering, passing, corner, free kick
- Further tactical education has to account for the actual manpower of the team

◄ V. Appendix ►

Garrison Trail-Running Competition

To conclude winter training, trail running competitions are to be held by the end of April for all garrisons. All companies, the battalion, division, regiment headquarters, cavalcades, intelligence corps, etc. of all parts of the troops (except the commanding staff) have to participate on the same day or under similar conditions.

Participation is mandatory for:

- All senior lieutenants and lieutenants if not sick or commandeered to another garrison,

- 80% of all non-commissioned officers from the unit's effective strength,

- 80% of the effective strength of all units.

- All men will be counted in their units' effective strengths except those:

  - Older than thirty

  - In their last year of service

  - Commandeered to another garrison

  - All other non-commissioned officers and men - the sick, those on holiday, etc. - are to be seen as part of the 20% released from the trail run. Sick or commandeered officers are to be released and not to be counted

Officers on holiday have to do the run shortly before or after their holiday and are to be counted. Officers, non-commissioned officers, and men not dispensable on the day of the trail run must do the run shortly before or after the garrison competition and are to be counted.

In addition to the 80% of draftable soldiers, all soldiers are allowed to compete. Their performances are to be counted as long as they improve the rating of their unit, meaning no matter the actual number of competing soldiers, only the best 80% of draftable soldiers will be counted. Officers, non-commissioned officers, and men can only replace soldiers of their own rank group.

Training: The garrison trail running competition requires appropriate training. This training should be comprised of 8 trial runs between November and the garrison competition in April. At least once in these trials, the soldier must run 5000m without pause.

On the day of the competition each unit has to notify the commanding officer in writing about those soldiers who haven't participated in at least 8 trial runs. These soldiers are to be released from the trail run on the day of the competition. They are to make good for those trial runs (no more than two runs per week). The garrison commander schedules the day on which they will do the actual run.

Course: The running track length shall be 5000m on varied terrain with small elevation differences. The start line needs to measure at least 30m across.

Start and finish should be on the same level and in close proximity.

The garrison commander determines the track by February 1st each year, announces it to the units and opens it up for trials. The garrison commander also determines the minimum time the soldiers have to complete the trail run.

For a track of 5000m without remarkable obstacles, a time of 22m30s shall serve as reference.

Scoring:

- Runners who finish within 15 seconds of each other will receive an equal score.

- Runners who finish in the minimum time required receive 0 points.

  (Example: assuming a minimum of 22 minutes 30 seconds, all runners who finish the run between 22 minutes 15.1 seconds and 22 minutes 30 seconds will receive 0 points)

- Runners who run slower than the required time will lose 2 points for every 15 seconds over the required minimum time, up to a maximum of minus 100 points.

- Runners finishing up to 5 minutes faster than the required minimum time will receive 1 bonus point for each 15 seconds under this limit.

  Assuming a minimum prescribed time of 22 minutes 30 seconds, those runners who finish between 17 minutes 15.1 seconds and 17 minutes 30 seconds will receive 20 bonus points.

  Those runners which exceed the minimum required time by more than 5 minutes earn 2 bonus points instead of 1 for every 15 seconds under the minimum time limit.

- 100 points will be subtracted for every man under the compulsory 80% effective strength. Absences during the run due to injury or sickness are still to be penalized with minus 100 points, if the absence means that less than 80%of the effective strength runs to the finish

- The unit with the highest average score is the winner. In case of a draw in points, the team with the higher percentage of runners who completed the course in less than the prescribed time wins.

- In the calculation of average scores, decimal points are only taken into account for units wherein every runner completed the course in less than the prescribed time.